In the Blink of an EYE

In the Blink *of an* EYE

MARY ELLEN EATON SMITH

In the Blink of an Eye

Copyright © 2019 by Mary Ellen Eaton Smith . All rights reserved.

No part of this publication may be reproduced, stored in a retrieval system or transmitted in any way by any means, electronic, mechanical, photocopy, recording or otherwise without the prior permission of the author except as provided by USA copyright law.

The opinions expressed by the author are not necessarily those of URLink Print and Media.

1603 Capitol Ave., Suite 310 Cheyenne, Wyoming USA 82001
1-888-980-6523 | admin@urlinkpublishing.com

URLink Print and Media is committed to excellence in the publishing industry.

Book design copyright © 2019 by URLink Print and Media. All rights reserved.

Published in the United States of America

ISBN 978-1-64367-880-1 (Paperback)
ISBN 978-1-64367-881-8 (Hardback)
ISBN 978-1-64367-879-5 (Digital)

23.09.19

I didn't ever see it coming, that your life could change in the blink of an eye. My name is Mary Ellen Eaton Smith and I am a stroke survivor. My stroke was on June 8th, 2008. I want to tell you about my story and my journey when I had my stroke, and how it began. I'm sure each one of you can relate to some of the things I am going to say, maybe it's a Stroke, Cancer, Diabetes, Dementia, Alzheimer's, Heart failure, Polio, Wounded Warriors amputees or something else that is life-threatening.

I was the eighth child born out of eleven children and I have been healthy, the biggest part of my life. I have raised three children, Stacey Jamison Lawson, Amy Jamison Smith, and Kenny Jamison. They are now grown up, with children of their own. My first marriage was about 26 years. I took care of my sick and dying husband for the last twelve years, before he passed away. I also had taken care of my mother-in-law for 20 years with her illness until she died.

My profession was being a Hair Designer over 45 years. The last place I worked: love my job and retired as Master Designer for 16 years was at JC Penney Styling Salon in Alton Illinois. I enjoyed doing my exercises; going to a gym and taking long walks. This helped me to relax at the end of the day. I was involved in church and sang in the choir. I enjoyed being the Chairman for the mother and daughter banquet in Medora Illinois at the First Baptist for six years. I love to travel, love to dance. I did volunteer work, loved walking with my daughter Amy, and with my associates for the March of Dimes sponsoring JCPenney. We also cut hair at JCPenney for money going to the Ronald McDonald house. I was a mime, portraying Jesus on the cross for three years performing at different events. Enjoyed life and most of all enjoying my husband, parents, children, grandchildren, my brothers and sisters and the rest of my family and friends.

𝒥n March of 2008, my sister Sue Eaton Bruce had been diagnosed with three aneurysms on the brain and was immediately recommend surgery. The doctor in St. Louis told her, all of her siblings should be checked out. Sue's first two surgeries on the brain, she went through that with flying colors. The third surgery didn't come out very well. The thing that happened. Sue had her last surgery and lost one eyesight. We both had surgery a week apart and mine ended being a major stroke. We were told later that Sue was in ICU for eight days and I was in for two weeks. Evidently, we talked to each other and said when we get out; we're going to go dancing and other silly things. Each one of us doesn't remember a thing about this. Kim Galanti; my niece and my daughter, said they were laughing so hard listening to our conversation.

Out of all of my sisters, Sue and I were the only two that had aneurysms on the brain. My younger sisters; Shirley Dunnagan and Barbara Odom, and my youngest brother Jesse Eaton had it checked out and they had none. The older ones, I don't really know if they had it checked.

I am originally from Illinois. I was born there; raised there, attended schools, and went to cosmetology college in Olney Illinois, which is known for the home of the white squirrels. My heart will always be in Illinois because of my children, grandchildren, family and friends. I became a widow after 26 years of marriage.

I remarried seven and one-half years later, to a man that I went to school with. I have known him since grade school. I will never forget; when I was in the fifth grade, we were at a sock hop at the grade school. The boys were on one side of the gym and the girls are on the other side. The chaperones put on a record called Sea Of Love. The young man came walking across the gym, he was the only one and all the girls were talking and said they wanted to know who is he going to pick—It was me. Who would ever believe after all those years have passed, we ended up getting married.

Since the doctor recommended to the family it would be best for all to have it checked out; my medical doctor, a resident in San Antonio, had sent me to be tested. I didn't feel that I had anything wrong but she said I should. She reported in a couple of days quickly that they discovered an aneurysm in my brain. She immediately recommended a neurologist who was considered to be one of the top doctors in San Antonio Texas. I felt a little hesitant, but finally decided to go see him and to get his opinion. I was very impressed with his bedside manner; he seemed concerned and so very nice. He talked to my husband and me, but recommended it should be my decision whether to have the surgery or not. He said he could see that I had taken good care of myself and looked healthy, and he didn't seem to think I would have any complications. The only thing if I had the surgery; he told me, my energy would be depleted and it would possibly take six to eight weeks to build my strength back up. He recommended for me to go home and think strongly about it. As we drove home; in my mind, I actually was afraid of thinking about it. The days passed, I decided not to have the surgery, thought it was best to just to keep having it checked. Approximately three weeks later the neurosurgeon called and talked to both of us. He thought that I really needed the surgery because of the history in my family. He again told me I was very healthy and felt I would be fine. I prayed about it and had decided to trust him at his word. I made a decision to go for it. I have many regrets now that I didn't get a second opinion. With having any surgery, I would recommend anyone to definitely get a second opinion. I have learned from this, but a bit too late for me.

They scheduled my surgery on a Monday. My three children and six grandchildren, and my stepfamily came to San Antonio to be there for me. I have been remembering good thoughts the day before the surgery, we had a BBQ at our house with my family and my husband's family and dear friends had joined us. It was a delightful day not worrying and having my faith in God, everything was going to be fine with having the major brain surgery. In the evening; we all went downtown San Antonio at Mi Tierra, ate Mexican food, and talked and laughed together. What a joyous time not expecting any problems to rise up!!!!

The following day came to drive to the hospital. We left at 5:30 in the morning en route for the day of my destiny. The nurse came in and gave me a shot to relax me, they gave me a pen and a paper to read and sign. Feeling the effects of the shot; I really didn't want to read it. But out of all the list on the paper which might happen, honestly, the word that actually stuck out at me was STROKE. I really didn't see anything else and now looking back, I truly believe that the Holy Spirit was trying to tell me something. I ignored it, but it was still in the back of my mind. I was at the hospital prepared for my surgery. It definitely was the day (I didn't see it coming)

The surgery was over, but much later my family was told there was a problem. I wasn't waking up. My doctor said he would give me more time to wake up, telling them everything went so well. Guess what? I wasn't waking up, then the doctor had told my family they were scheduling me in a few hours for more tests. He had told them. "She might have had a stroke during surgery". After more test was done, he told them he had mistakenly clipped the small vessels right beside the aneurysm, causing me to have a stroke. I definitely had a bad surgery that went very wrong. As a result, I did have a MAJOR STROKE.

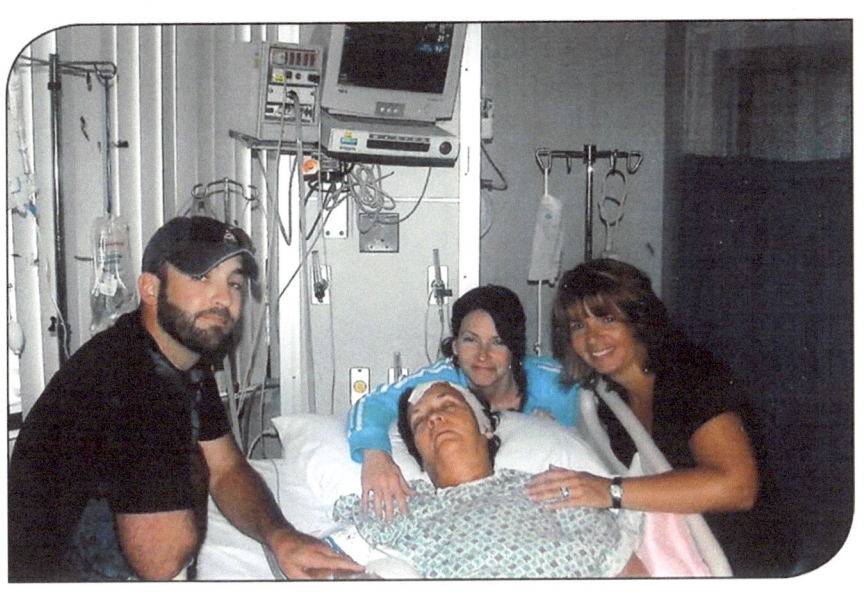

Picture of my three children after my Stroke, Kenny Jamison, Amy Jamison Smith, and Stacey Jamison Lawson

I don't remember anything but was told later that they kept me in intensive care for approximately two weeks, and then moved me to a rehab hospital for five weeks. When I was brought into ICU that day, the nurse had told my husband that two people had died that day earlier. One man was at Sea World on vacation from California having a great time with his family and young children had passed away from a heart attack. Another man sick had died too... Thank God I survived, God spared me. My doctor wanted me to be carefully watched, and the nurse told my husband that she didn't want to see the third death happen to another family. After my long stay in ICU, they transferred me to a rehab but I don't remember anything about the ride.

This was where the nightmare started! I woke up in a bed in a rehab hospital thinking I was just having a very bad dream. When I tried to move my right side that was my dominant side, it felt like hundreds of pounds were holding me down, nothing moved. I couldn't even feel the right side of my arm, leg, face, or head. I felt so confused and helpless. I honestly didn't know if this was a dream or was this really happening. I thought again was I dreaming or was it real. I thought that I heard my girls saying to the nurse who was trying to weigh me, they said she can't stand up she had a major stroke. Was it a bad dream or was it real? When I was laying there I thought, "Oh dear lord, please let it be a horrible dream". I wanted to wake up from this terrible dream, but the reality was finally settling in, it was definitely not a dream. It was real for sure. Dear God what had happened to me was all that ran through my mind.

I had been moved to a floor that was being remolded, the construction men who were working there, they had the radio going full blast, they also had a trip hammer going and I heard them talking loud and with some laughter all day long! They had the outside big doors open which made the room; I was in, so cold. To me things just kept getting worse. I wanted to get up and jump out of the bed and go home. I sure didn't want to face what had happened and definitely started filling very depressed. Then again; I was actually hoping it was a dream and a terrible nightmare, and here I lay filling very trapped in the bed. I couldn't stop thinking, make it go away it really can't be happening, why doesn't this bad dream go away.

The day would start around 4:30 every morning. The aid would come in and actually slam me in the wheelchair, slam me on the toilet, slam me back in the wheelchair, slam me back in bed, get me dressed for the day, cover me up and then turn the lights out. The next thing was I was not able to go back to sleep and just laid in bed feeling trapped and became more depressed. She was definitely rough with me. I felt so very degraded by the way she treated me. I have never in years, ever slept in my street clothes. I had never been treated that way by anyone. I knew with her attitude and being rough with me, she sure hated life and her job!! Finally came time for breakfast and honestly eating was the farthest thing from my mind. I had no interest in eating or having hunger at any time. They would bring the food in: take off the lid and then leave without helping me to open the cream for my coffee, or juice, butter my toast or cut the meat with any meal. I actually felt I couldn't do it with depression—decreasing energy and losing the strength. Feeling the horrible weight of my dominant side, I felt so helpless. I just wanted everybody to leave me alone. I certainly had bad thoughts that I was experiencing and I never thought this could be happening to me with my life-changing. I actually had no desire to live. Who would feel like facing the day, not knowing if this is the way you were going to be for the rest of your life. My heart goes out to disabled people, which something happens to them and all they have to endure and go through. I finally got up the nerve and brazen enough to ask the nurse if I could have a different aid to help me. This certainly made me think how some elderly folks are treated in a nursing home without the family knowing it. When they can't speak for themselves. When they are treated ugly this way and sometimes with their minds, they can't report it. It breaks my heart to think of the elder, wonderful people going thru this and not able to tell anyone. I'm not saying all nursing homes are like this but I have heard some terrible stories before. Something just happened to them but they are still the same person. It sure takes their dignity away! They got me a different aid and she was full of compassion. I found out later the new aid was a sister to the one that was rough with me. Just thinking about how one can be so mean and the other one so sweet and compassionate. Even though she was nice and treated me like I was human. I still felt worthless and deeply depressed that I didn't want to live.

My roommate kept talking all the time repeating herself over and over. My nerves were shot and I just wanted to be left alone. Then her family would come in and there would be 10 to 15 people at one time laughing, and joking caring on. My feeling was ready to jump out of my body. I had always been a caring people-person but believe me, my mind and attitude had really changed. I sure didn't like myself at all.

As Donnie and my stepdaughter Eugina came to see me and be with me for the day, he told me I'm taking you out for a ride and to go eat. I didn't want to go knowing I was going to face people outside of the rehab. He got a wheelchair and insisted that I go. I had so much anger in me but I tried to get through it. We went to eat at a place by our house, called Aldaco's. The owner came out and unlocked the chain so they could get my wheelchair in. I wanted to go in the back way of the restaurant. Talk about feeling embarrassed; I wanted to hide, I can remember bits of it but then I can't remember the ride back to the rehab. It was another miserable day and I wanted to get back in bed and hide from reality.

Couple times I had dear friends come in to see me, Robert and Jodie Duron come in and Donnie had rolled me out in the garden in my wheelchair. It was a few days after I was in rehab. I don't remember at all talking to them it's such a burr. Also, a later date Gary and Wanda Lawson came to see me and I remember Gary bent over and kissed my foot that was paralyzed. My heartfelt like it dropped from his great kindness. Another date comes to my mind Diane and Emily Brucato and some of their family came to visit me when all of a sudden one of Diane's granddaughters passed out. I hope seeing me was not the cause of it.

I had therapy twice a day, but they didn't even work with my right arm at all. It sure needed the attention, my mind was not thinking at the time to ask them if they were going to work with my paralyzed arm. I was told later that I have to treat the problem as soon as I can, and not ignore this, I have to try and reroute my brain.

They had me putting puzzles together with my left hand which was not my dominant side. I told them as a kid I didn't like puzzles then and I don't like them now, which made them laugh, but I was dead serious. I felt my body and personality had definitely changed for the bad. I didn't realize that they were testing to see if I had any memory left, at that time my mind was a little fuzzy, but thank God I did. I wasn't completely thinking straight the way that I did before the surgery. The other therapist was trying to make me learn to walk, they were sweet and very nice people. I had to laugh at myself, I remember I was trying to chew gum and all of a sudden it disappeared. The compassionate therapist, I said to her, I can't find my gum. She quickly answered and said Mary Ellen, honey it's hanging on your lip. I was also embarrassed feeling stupid since I couldn't feel the side of my face or lips that all. I really think that was the first time I had since I had the stroke to smile at myself!!! My first days of physical therapy in Texas I was trying to learn how to walk. The Physical therapist, a very nice young lady, was helping me. I was only able to take a couple of steps. She told me that my muscles would not get strong unless I keep walking not to get a brace. She said never get a brace for your leg. Then when we came back to Illinois, I started therapy in Illinois the first thing that a therapist said was that I needed a brace. Well not knowing and my memory wasn't all that clear, he recommended I need to get an AFO. He measured my foot and ordered me a brace. I went to therapy and I struggled with this with pain for months. We left Illinois and went back to Texas, and I started therapy there and I was still having difficulty walking for a year and a half. I had lived through so much pain and anxiety. The therapist recommended that I go to the University of Texas medical center to an individual there, to take a look at the problem on my foot. The first thing Tom said that using this brace was for a very big man. It was three times bigger than what I should have. That was my problem, and had been wearing it for a year and a half; this is no wonder I was having so much trouble walking. So the point I'm trying to make is that I struggled with a problem that was no fault of my own. I could have been farther in walking, if I would have listened to the first therapist telling me not to get a brace. But when I came back to Illinois, they told me I needed a brace. You really don't know what's going to happen because nobody is perfect and we all make mistakes, people make mistakes all the time. The only thing I can say is I wouldn't have endured a year and a half of complete pain. One tells me not to get a brace and another tells me I needed it. I wished that I had listened to the first therapist but I didn't. Just wanted to get better and be me again.

I went through 5 weeks of speech therapy, and it was so boring. Of course, anything I had to do, my heart was not in it? I did have to learn to pronounce several words better which made me irritable and the therapist got on my nerves. An hour of this every day was hard to take. It was not her fault, bless her heart; it was me with my state of mind! Later as I was back in my room lying flat on my back thinking of her. I actually thought; Mary Ellen don't be mad or mean, God does not want you to be that way. I definitely wanted to try to -Be Nice and Humble!

Thank the Good Lord I could talk but sometimes the words would come out wrong. I have to say I laugh about it now. This was very frustrating but I had to try to retrain my brain. More challenges definitely were to learn to try to use my left hand to get dressed with the dead weight of my right side. I felt worthless, for I couldn't do the things I once did before and thinking that we all do take life for granted. I finally was released from rehab and Donnie asked a nurse if they would have a sling for my right arm. The nurse who worked in a different unit asked what was wrong with my arm. My husband told her she had a stroke on her right side. She could not believe that they did not work with my arm on my dominant side all the time I was there.

The day I was released my husband took me to go to see the surgeon who had operated on me. Of course, I was in a wheelchair, could not walk. I felt like my right side really wasn't there. I felt like I had lost my leg and arm. I really felt degraded, ugly, feeling discouraged and so miserable in other words; I became more depressed. I didn't care to put on any make-up, my hair wasn't fixed, I wasn't dressed very well. Being a Hair Designer for years and as a child, we were taught to take care of our selves. We were definitely brought up that way from our dear sweet mother. But to tell you the truth, I really didn't care anything about my life at that moment. I sure did not like myself at all!!!

When we arrived at the doctor's office; in my wheelchair he completely ignored me, like I wasn't even in the room. His conversation was directed just to my husband. He didn't even look or acknowledge me, it was like I was invisible and I wasn't even there. As we were getting ready to leave the office; he barely looked at me and in his cold voice, he finally acknowledged me and said (you need to get up Mrs. Smith and walk walk walk very stern) The words that came out of his mouth hurt so bad, I felt so again degraded, like what's wrong with you doctor, are you kidding me! After all, you made this terrible mistake and put me in this shape. To hear the hurtful things out of his mouth; I couldn't walk at all, filling my dominant side weighing a ton. He wasn't the pleasant man that was so kind and so nice to me. It was a different man before he did the surgery. I know that in my heart if he would have said he was sorry, and acted like I was a human being that this happened, and felt bad, I would have felt a little better about him. I would have respected him and learn in time to forgive him because no one is perfect and make mistakes. The only one that is perfect is our Heavenly Father. I've grown up with wonderful parents who taught all of us kids to learn to forgive others. This treatment to me made me feel that he knew what he had done, that his actions to me was not being a caring man. He made my mind started thinking negative and that I would always be this way and I was not going to heal. This action of his—cold treatment wasn't positive to me, thinking again with heartache, he's the one that had made the terrible mistake. This made me more depressed than ever and felt more helpless and again, I lost all hope in my life.

Finally arrived home after receiving the bad experience with the doctor, I was ready to go to bed. I knew I could only lay flat on my back. There wasn't a chance in the world I could even turn on each of my sides to be somewhat comfortable. The good thing about this was I actually liked being in bed. I felt like I could hide trying not to accept what had happened to me. I felt it sure was an escape from reality. How could I feel any encouragement when I couldn't even move!!

In a few weeks, Donnie made arrangements to take me back to Illinois to be around my family and friends. He also needed an escape from it all because it was surely a bad life change for him also. One thing he loved me and I had been blessed by an angel. He sure didn't turn his back on me. The flight was a nightmare to be facing people who stare, some who pretend you're not there, and people thinking you must not be in your right mind. I really think some people seeing you're handicapped so they think your mind is handicapped. This was where my pride and self-worth came in, boy what an adjustment!!! There were several people in wheelchairs to get on the plane. I was at the end of the wheelchairs, Donnie was standing behind me and this man said to him, "This is pitiful these people in these wheelchairs slows everything down." Without hesitation, my husband turned around and said to him, don't you think she would rather be in your spot standing, than where she's at right now. The heartless ill-mannered man didn't say another word. Most people are caring but then there are people who are not!!!

My two daughters Stacey and Amy met us at the St. Louis Airport and drove us to our summer home in Holiday Shores. I will never forget the wonderful site that I saw– there were six of my seven grandchildren lined up, from the eldest down to the youngest, waiting with big hugs and kisses. Cole Lawson, Kaitlyn Lawson, Blake Lawson, Kylor Smith, Kody Smith, and Rylee Smith. When I had the stroke my granddaughter was born to my son Kenny and Callea Jamison. Kenlea had trouble coming into the world. Later on, my son wrote a song with the heartache from his wife's pregnancy and me having a stroke. He wrote a song (In The Hands Of Christ) If you want to hear it go to Song " Kenny Jamison- Hands Of Christ" listen online @ Tidido.com from his album Anywhere with You. It brought tears to my eyes. He is a songwriter and a singer. Seeing my grandchildren, I felt a great joy came over me since my life had changed. I felt so thankful to God for being alive. I realized and prayed then I was going to fight to get better and never give up. Seeing my grandchildren and the wonderful feeling going off my shoulders like the angels were lifting away the pain, to give it to God and keep my faith and work hard to get better.!!!!

Another beautiful thing happened that made me feel better as I was home in Illinois. I received over 200 get-well cards and flowers and gifts. I am so thankful to all my dear family and friends. They brought us food and even came to the house to prepare the table and food. Thank you everyone; you have no idea how you all made me feel. I sure want to thank each and every one of you. I have to say that one thing that hurt me bad; was friends that I thought were really my friends, weren't. Many people will walk in and out of your life but true friends leave footprints in your heart. Maybe they couldn't deal with it!!! I will give them the benefit of the doubt!!!

Time had passed then a few weeks later, I had decided it was time again to sign up for therapy to get better, and quit feeling sorry for myself. I was told and recommended a place close to my house. They evaluated me and they were very nice therapists. One of the therapists went out of her way to do anything she could to help me. Several weeks at this facility, later I was told by one of the therapists, I would have to accept the way it was. There was nothing she could do to help me. In other words; it made me think no matter what I did, I was going to be in the wheelchair and handicapped for the rest of my life, and that's the way it will be. Well needless to say; that set me back, I became very heartbroken and depressed so I canceled completely my therapy. Hearing this from a professional therapist it crushed me very much. She sure didn't encourage me, I thought that they were there to encourage you not degrade you. Hearing this made me ready to give up, I actually really felt that the devil was so happy for me to feel this way. To tell you the truth again at that time, I didn't care.

After a few weeks, my husband tried to encourage me to go somewhere else. I was very much reluctant; I started praying that if I would try again, God will send me to Godly therapists. I really needed to remember the feeling that I had when I saw my Grandchildren. God was telling me not to give up and to have faith. Later on, a friend who recommended me to a different facility told me it was the office staff of St. Claire's in Alton Illinois. The office workers were so wonderful just talking to them on the telephone. They sure encouraged me to come in. They met me and made me feel good to join the outpatient therapy. I was very satisfied and felt overwhelmed thru their kindness and definitely felt God had really sent me there. The office staffs, Rose Small and Kim Pavish, were so wonderful and made me feel welcomed. The therapists Carol Babcock, Debbie Fisher, Jim Stewart, Kelly Bogowith made me feel so confident the way they all were so positive; making me feel that I have a chance to get better. Debbie was always such a big cut up and loved to hear her funny stories, which made me and Carol laugh so much. To laugh is the greatest way to heal. When Carol started the therapy on me, my right arm was tight to my chest and couldn't even budge it—let alone straighten it out. This was so painful; but we laughed so much, the positions that she tried to relax it, oh my gosh we needed a camera. Kelly and Jim were excellent too and a lot of fun, which made the therapy and hard work, come along better. I really felt like they were all guardian Angels, that God had sent me there. I felt like my mind was healing some and I was able to laugh more than cry.

We had met our neighbors next door at our house in Holiday Shores. Red and Teresa Smith are originally from Ponchatoula. Red works in the Oil industry and other places and Teresa is his right arm working along beside him. We got acquainted with them and love both of them. Red and Donnie took me down to our boat in my wheel chair. I was a little bit scared when this happened because of the steep hill. We took a nice ride in our boat and enjoyed their company. I was a little scared and worried thinking about them taking me back up the steep, of course, I didn't tell them. They got a little bit off track when they rolled me up. I remember Teresa yelling to be careful. Yay, we made it through the challenge with a lot of laughter and prayer. We have become dear friends and we feel like they are more than family than friends including their children and grandchildren. I know God put them in our life and I'm so grateful for this.

We decided to travel back to Texas to our residence for a while. My husband was getting the wheelchair out of the car. I had made up my mind I'm going to work without the wheelchair and he said, you need it. Of course, I did, but I felt thru God and my faith and my stubbornness were going to help me to get out of it. It wasn't easy, it was a struggle. One thing that I can say my grandchildren had a lot of fun with the wheelchair, the boys popped willies.

One day Donnie and I decided to go down on the River Walk in Texas to get some exercise. I had a lot of difficulties walking as I was holding on to him. There were three couples sitting at a table watching me walk. Of course, my pride rose up and like I said, was down on myself. I stopped in my tracks and said to them. Yes, I had a stoke but I'm walking. To my surprise, they started clapping. It made me try to remember and not forget there are more caring people out there than negatives ones. I should have remembered to try to be always, more humble and kind.

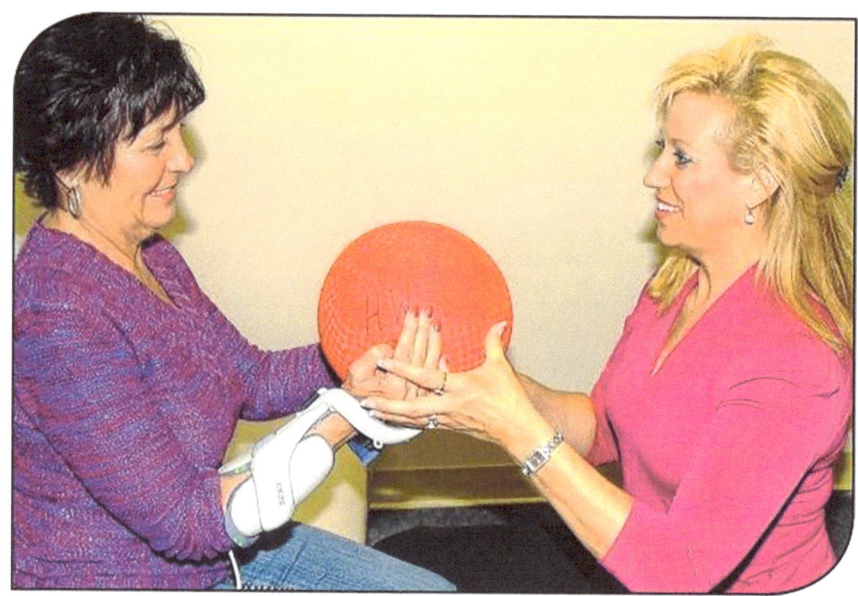

We came back to Illinois the latter part of June for a few months. I signed up again at Saint Claire's, I just can't seem to stay away from their encouraging words and the patience they have with their patients. I continued my exercise and tried to do what they tell me now for several months. I can say it is not always easy and many times I get tired and want to give up but that is a short thought, you have to stay positive because the negative and the devil will slip in there to discourage you if you dwell on it. God is within me, I will not fail. My speech still needed work so I started singing different songs on a CD that my husband had made me, and also on the radio. It helps me a lot and I will always continue doing it, and will not stop, this had helped me tremendously with my speech.

I was asked from St. Clair's rehab if I would be interested in being introduced to an e- stem called the Bioness with Carol Babcock. I was so happy to have this opportunity and felt like I would do anything to get better. It is not God, but thank God, he gave men and women the intelligence to invent this e-stem to help get stoke survivors stronger. I could see that it works but you have to work with it, it helps you to connect a new path to the brain. It makes your hand and fingers relax and keep your hand from going into a fist.

I was very blessed to be a part of Saint Claire's rehab in Alton Illinois—remembering they were so good to me. They are a group that really cares for their patients. I was blessed to be involved talking to other stroke survivors, to try and encourage them how much the Bioness has helped me. I was also very blessed which they had put in the paper about me using the Bioness, I was very blessed also to be in two health magazines, one going up to Chicago hospital about stroke survivors. I felt like this all was in God's work. I love to talk to survivors because no one knows the heartache, the depression, the no self-worth, and not knowing the feeling if you haven't been there. When I'm in Illinois; sometimes. I go to therapy and talk and try to encourage someone that recently had a stroke and very depressed. People don't realize the work we have to do in trying to retrain the brain and try to get better. Some people that I've seen just give up and I pray for them to try and get better. Many want to get better but some are paralyzed for life, or blinded by the stroke or makes them where they cannot talk, and they are trapped in their own bodies. Whenever I see someone who have stroke: on the television or radio, it breaks my heart because I know how they feel. I remember seeing Dick Clark, Kirk Douglas and many others who had strokes. Stroke is a painful, mean and very degrading thing!

I can say I have tried to stay positive, if you're negative you can't get better. Sometimes I would do so good, I would take four steps forward and then again two steps back. I would try so hard, through my faith to not let it bother me when people stare. I love people but another time I remember those hurtful times. One time as Donnie and I walked into an Orange Leaf Ice Cream Parlor; I was still having trouble walking, the outside tables were full of people but I sadly remember one woman who stared me down from the top of my head to my feet. The closer I got to her she really looked me over. I felt so humiliated, ugly, and saddened. She was so disrespectful; hurtful which made me think, God, please forgive me for feeling negative to this lady. They don't have a clue what I am going through and I hope it never happens to her.

When I go out to eat at a restaurant and see people in their wheelchair, I can't resist not going up to them and asking how they are doing. My husband says don't bother them. I want to show my love for them. You would not believe the look and smile on their faces. They are the same people, but just had something happened to them. I realize some people have no idea what you're going through and I try to understand it. If it were a child looking which they're wondering what's is wrong with her, I understand that, but when grown-ups act in a rude way, it makes my pride seems to go out the door. I'm wondering if a lot of people that have problems feel the same way that I feel. I have been told not to let it bother me; but, they do not have to deal with the hurt. I pray one of these days I will get past it! To tell you the truth it made me sad again and brought on depression. I prayed, dear God please help me.

Another story that happened, but I hope it makes you laugh. I could not drive my car yet, so Donnie took me to therapy and then picked me up. We had decided to stop and eat on the beltline in Alton Illinois to have Chinese food. We were standing alone waiting for a table when a large crowd came in behind us. This guy behind me said in a real loud (what did you do to your arm?) I looked at him and people behind him are looking and listening. I meant to say I had an aneurysm on my brain, had surgery, the doctor admitted that he made a mistake. He clipped vessels by my aneurysm. So I woke up from a stroke paralyzed on my dominant side, but that is not what I had said, this is what I did say. "I had surgery on my brain for an aneurysm; the neurosurgeon performed the surgery and when I woke up I was pregnant". My husband looked at me like, "what did you just say". The people were staring at me, like what's wrong with that woman is she crazy? And I could not stop laughing. I should have shocked them since they were gazing at me and said, "yep that's a good doctor". Even as we sat down to have our food I could not eat because of laughing so hard at myself. That sure was a good medicine for me but I guess the people thought different.

We started traveling again even though I still was not in good shape, but I was too stubborn to give up. We made a trip to Chicago with our dear friends: Paul and Pearl Flaman. Donnie wanted to get me a wheelchair because there would be a lot of walking. Trying to stay positive, silently I asked Dear God please please help me to be able to walk. Through my faith, we walked on the Navy Pier and to different sites. I walked 3 1/2 miles feeling worn out. Thank God that was the farthest I have walked in a day since my stroke in 2008.

Well here I go again, As I was heading to a stroke survivor meeting at Saint Claire's hospital, I was walking through the door with my cane and my brace on my leg. I got halfway through the heavy door, and it came back on me. It knocked me down tossed me around like a rag doll, I had hit my face and head. Immediately, I had a bad headache. It continually tossing me around and I came down on my left knee, which became a large knot right away. Security was called and checked everything out and security said the door did not register with my weight. I didn't understand that. I was not able to catch myself because my right side was too weak. They asked me if I wanted to go to the emergency room: but with my stubbornness and embarrassment, I would not go.

Sometimes your pride overpowers to making the right decision, this is a picture of how my face was bruised.

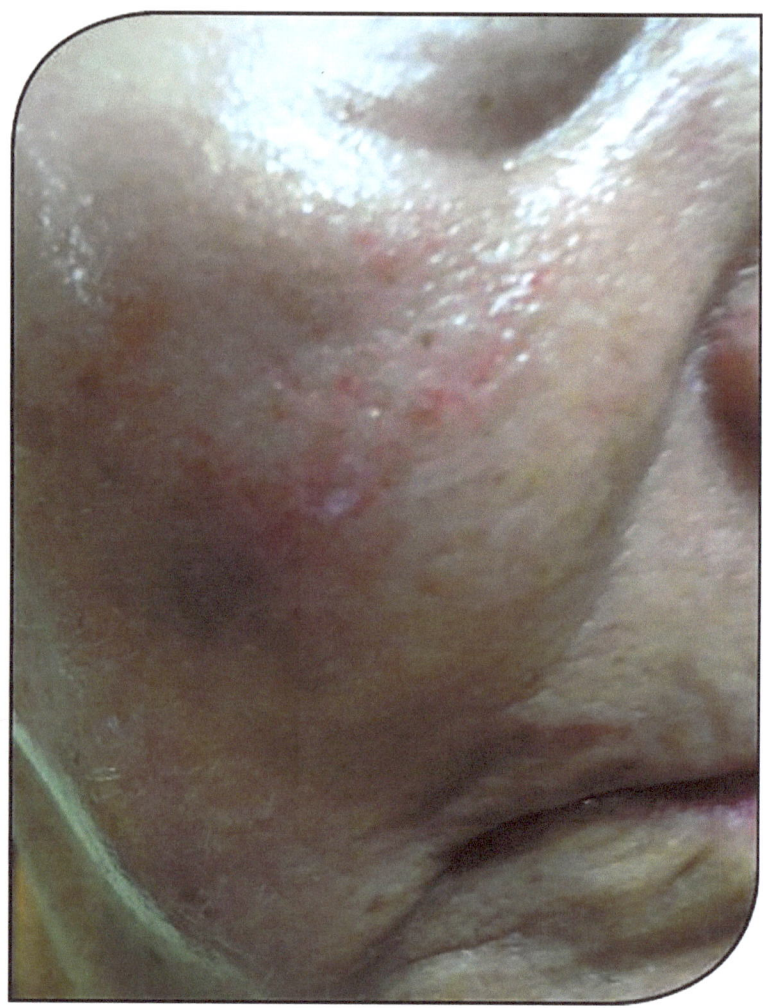

Being healthy and then your life changed in the blink of an eye, you never can dream how it makes you feel. I felt like I had taken ten steps forward and then I took five steps back again. But thank God that we have him to talk to. I know he is by my side all the time. Faith goes from a small beginning to a grand finale.

My bruise on my face when I hit the wall !! As time passed, I felt trapped in my house not being able to drive. My husband said call your family or friends to take you around. I have always been independent and didn't want to bother anyone. After two years, I decided to get a hold of a Special person that took stroke survivors for a test in the car, to see if you're able to drive. I did a lot of praying to the Lord. Faith continues when we hold onto the promise. I was very nervous because I had to drive with my left foot and guide with my left hand since I was born right-handed. Another big challenge; but with God's help and determination, I was able to get my license to drive again. It was challenging to learn to drive with the opposite side. I was very nervous but with God's help, I was able to do it. I mastered it and had no problem. I consider my left side now to always be my stronger side.

Even though I work so hard to get better, I realize you have to accept what it is and not to be bitter. You have to stay positive and honestly, I didn't for quite a while. It's easier said than done, but that's the only way that you can heal. I make myself to do certain exercises every morning and ride a stable bike to exercise my legs. Now I have bought a three-wheeler and with God's help, I will try to ride in my subdivision. One day I decided I was so bored in the house that I drove to Walmart to walk around and get some exercise. Of course, I used one of the baskets to push because of my weak right side. I was walking around and my phone rang and it was my son Kenny calling to see how I was doing, and what I was doing. I told him I've been walking around three hours in Walmart. He sounded serious and said mom are you all right? I told him I'm fine, and this made me laugh. My kids seem to be overprotective to me, just like I was always to them, maybe a little too much.

I was invited by my daughter; Amy, to come to her gym in Brighton Illinois to talk to her Boot Camp. I love to try to talk to people and encourage them to never give up and to trust in the Lord because he is there for us. I pray some of my words to stroke survivors; or anything else, I hope this will encourage them. I have to say my faith is what keeps me going and to never give up!

I do my E-Stem several times a week on my right hand. Type on the iPad left-handed and practice as much as possible. The more you work it sometimes gets a lot easier and I'm sure that things happen to people. They know what I'm saying, to work hard and keep your faith.

I had a very hard time forgiving and it hurts deeply for the doctor that did my surgery, the way I was treated by him after I had my stroke. I finally typed him a letter and told him that I forgive him; no one is perfect except God. I felt like I had to do this to heal myself. My husband sent it first class and I know that he received it. I knew in my heart that I wouldn't hear from him. I felt like I had to let go and not feel sorry for myself. This was the beginning of my forgiving and to stop being so bitter. My favorite verse is (In all thy ways acknowledge him and he shall direct your path) he is there if you keep your faith and call on him, he never leaves us.

I went to therapy for four years off and on, now I do exercise at home. I go to the store at HEB in Texas and walk to get exercise holding on to a cart. I do the same at Walmart in Illinois, I walked there for a couple of hours. It makes me really tired but also I can feel that I'm getting stronger. I drive myself to the stores and all over San Antonio, which is a challenge, believe me with the traffic. It is so different learning to drive with the opposite of your dominant side. It made me think. I now cut my husband's hair with my left hand. Actually, I can do things that I've always done, but I've learned to do it with my opposite side. If someone tells me that's too hard for you, believe me, I can do it by my determination and a lot of praying to God for helping me, and I certainly feel the strength he is giving me. I feel God is helping me I am now confident with my driving and I feel safe behind the wheels and everything I do in my house, I'm beginning to dance slow and am working on moving faster to dance. I will get there sooner or later. I'm a firm believer that it is in Gods time that I will feel more confident. I also have been walking barefooted in my house with my brace off. I started out slow and believe me: no matter how you constantly work to get better, it sure is a slow process. I will master it someday. You cannot give up and if anyone is reading my book and have a problem, please keep trying and keep your faith because God is right by our side. He knows our name, he knows our every thoughts, He sees each tear that falls, and I know he hears when we call.

When you see people out that are in a wheelchair, don't be afraid to speak to them, or someone walking with difficulty. You never know if you're life will change In The Blink Of An Eye!

We are back to traveling and enjoying life. I still deal with my stroke, and still have the pain. I feel like no one can make me feel inferior without my permission: steal my sense of value, they can't change who you are, unless you allow them to. The best thing that helped me was trying to be patient, trying to stay as positive as much as you can. People have no idea what you are going through. My Faith is what drives me never to give up. We take the simple things in life for granted. I do know without God in my life, I could not be this far. Also with my Family and Friends, the wonderful therapist: Carol Babcock, Debbie Fisher, Kelly Bogowith, Jim Stewart, and the office workers. Learn to give is more important than receiving; I'm in control of my destiny. God has a plan for all of us. You don't know how to live until you almost die. My whole perspective changed. I have a lot more sympathy for people with the things that have happened to them. Learn to laugh more, especially at yourself.

Today I went to the grocery store in Texas and walked for three hours for more exercise and of course, I grocery shopped. The only bad thing about this was I picked up things I really didn't need and should never buy. I was in line to check out, a handsome young man was checking out. His left arm was missing, we started a conversation and I told him my right arm is useless. He smiled and laughed at me, making the comment that we both know what it's like to only have one arm to use. He was a very pleasant man. We both laughed, it sure is better than crying.

So again, I see so much to be thankful for because the man has to go around the rest of his life without his arm. At least I have my arm but he has to bear people look at him. When we look around, some people are definitely worse off than we are. But I could tell: that sure didn't get him down and wondering what happened to him that he had an attitude. That was, in my opinion, he definitely is a child of God. Again you cannot give up on yourself, but I still have times when I get down, but it sure doesn't last very long.

We took another trip to Florida to see family, that had been very sick. We felt honored to fly with wounded Warriors, these men were headed to go scuba diving, they all had prosthetic a leg. They were having a great time laughing and were so pleasant, one soldier told me they had bicycled over 200 miles. What an encouragement when they were together, made me think the trials they are going through the rest of their lives. I saw their attitude was to never give up, they sure gave me a testimonial that I will never forget. All the people on the plane gave them loud applause.

This Memorial Day May of 2016, we went to Austin Texas and stayed there for 5 days. We have a boat and had it docked, as hoping to go out on the Travis Lake. The rain, came down and there were places flooded. We were blessed to get on the water, as only two days were sunny. Where our boat was docked, there were unbelievable steps to get to it. Hanging on with one hand and my right leg weak, I again had faith that God would give me the strength to go down the steps and then climb up. It was scary but l mastered it. I don't know which one was more challenging: going down the stairs or coming back up.

Here is a picture of some of the stairs up above we had to go down to the dock and then climb back up. It actually was in mid-air with nothing but water underneath it. This again, I was able to master these stairs. Again I give all the glory to our savior who has helped me so much!

As the years have passed since my Stroke, I endured the Doctor admittedly told my family that he made a mistake by clipping vessels around my Aneurysm, causing a Stoke completely on my dominant side from the top of head to the bottom of my foot.

Today I have come so far with a lot of work and exercise; doing it myself not going to therapy and I gave all my glory to Jesus Christ. I make myself, to go into a store holding on to a cart and walk, walk, walk. I always run into some of my school friends or neighbors at the store and always give me praise.

I have such wonderful family, school friends, neighbors, mostly my family who have stood by me, but some people that I don't know, look me up and down as I walk. Sometimes I want to say to them, your life can change ((In the Blink of An Eye) but then I try to ignore it and I'm not the kind of person who wants sympathy yet sympathetic to my fellow.

The family I can't afford losing. They were with me during the roller-coaster ride and I am more than thankful to have them with me. Cheers!

Traveling back memory lane, I used to hear my parents tell me "No man is an Island". Never did I truly understand the phrase until I've reached the rock bottom of my life. All the obstacles and tribulations are life-changing – it made me question God, but it also made me realize that everything truly has a reason. God made me experience all these things because he wants me to believe in him and to intensify my faith to him.

No man is an island indeed, and without these people who were on my side, making me push myself to my limits; I wouldn't have made it to the point of realization. I could have been a woman of sadness and pain. I could have been someone who believes I am all alone forever. These people are the reasons why I moved forward and saw a glass-half-full.

The subtleness of life is challenging and yet rewarding. In the midst of accepting all the hardships and moving forward from the stroke, I have had. Another unexpected heartache I didn't see coming. I thought the man-made stroke I have experienced is the most painful, however, this I believe is more heart-crunching.

Every Family has heartbreaks, and all my family has recently been heartbroken with a Shock to our bodies and her husband, sons, grandchildren, and daughter-in-law.

My 69-year-old sister Barbara Odom died from a Heart attack and lived 25 days.

We all sisters are very close to each other. We were taught that no matter what happens, we should all stick together and support each other along the way. The time I knew that she died, I couldn't explain the thoughts in my mind. All the memories we've had together with our sisters were flashing back to my memory. Barbara who is very close to me died – at first, I couldn't accept it. I just told myself that it should be a nightmare, a very bad nightmare. But when I realized that she really is dead, I cried like a wolf. I couldn't sleep even how stressful my day was, it is unbelievable. My faith again was tested!

During the wake, my family and friends' moral supports were at its apex. They never showed weariness in extending their deepest condolences to my family. The faith that was tested now is back to its original intensity.

I believed that Barbara may be gone, but she will always remain in everyone's hearts. Barbara's friends, family, neighbors know that she is a phenomenal woman who shows kindness and speaks justice for everybody. She is a strong sister who is very willing to fight on her sisters' behalf. I know that she fought for her life, but I think God's will is to take her from us. It is truly painful, but I didn't have the choice but to accept that my sister, my very loving sister is no longer with me.

It ached my aorta seeing her in repose, my tears just fell down without me knowing it–**the pain is indescribable.**

During the last day of her wake, everybody showed their love to Barbara which I really have appreciated. Truly, when someone is good to others, they will get back to you and reciprocate the kindness you showed to them. My sister Barbara is such a great person who respects others, and now that she's gone, her friends stood up with us to extend support and love to her. We believe, that **her absence makes her present in our hearts.**

Mary Ellen Eaton Smith

When I think of you
I cry but I do not mind.
Because each teardrop
Is for you...
And each teardrop
Brings a memory
And each memory
Brings a smile.

—Ian Robertson

The death of my dear sister, Barbara, brought back all the painful moments I have had the time my other siblings died. I know that we all will come to the point of leaving the world, however, during those times I didn't quite understand why they left me.

Jimmy wearing the yellow cap and Don Eaton wearing an eyeglass together with my eldest sister, Jeanne.

My brothers Jimmy and Don Eaton died due to natural death. They were the epitome of strength not only to their own families but even to ours starting from the time we were still kids. They used to protect us from the other kids who tried to mock us. Though they showed gumption, they still are very kind to other kids. Such kindness has been on their blood up until they had their own families and trained their own kids. Their death knocked me down, but I always have thought about what they always have told me and my other siblings that we just have to be strong no matter what will happen.

Pain is like a shadow that has been haunting me for years which I didn't know but is like a monster that awakened after what happened to Barbara. There were nights that my brothers and sisters who already are in heaven, communicated with me through dreams. I woke up with an ache in my heart and my tears just fell down without me knowing.

As I look at this picture I have together with all my siblings, I just couldn't imagine the happiness inside me yet the sadness can't just be ignored. Sometimes I wish to see all of us having fun together once again. I miss my brothers and sisters, and I just hope to see them soon.

Time ran so fast since my Sister Barb Odom passed away. When I received this flower there were 3 large Pods in the plant and they had died and I cut them out and have been babying this 🌱. We all have grieved over losing her and still do, yesterday I was shocked to see one pod Behind Angel's head. Some people don't believe in this but, my Pastor told me stories how people have told him many things happened to a loved one after they had lost a loved one.

The same thing happened when my deceased husband Kenny Jamison died. I was so surprised to see one Pod because there were Three large Pods. This is only one growing again Maybe some people will laugh at this but, I feel Barb wants to tell us all she is ok 🙏

 I am feeling so sad thinking about my sister Barb Odom today and her husband, sons, grandchildren, and Trish. I look at this plant and baby it every day, it makes me cry. It's growing beautifully just like I know that Barb is up with the Angels and the Family. It was sent to me with love.

 I am thinking about my brothers and sisters who I miss very much. We leaned on each other and our many talks would say things to each other and if we didn't agree, we never got mad and didn't speak to each other. We never would try to hurt each other by making smart remarks to each other. Like I say, Family is indeed important. I was thinking we should all be for each other because we never know when we leave this world. The love for each other is so important.

 I have no doubt that they are in Glory with Jesus.

Thinking about my brothers and sisters who already passed away, I thought about visiting my eldest sister who I also dearly love.

Recently my Neice Sherry Throne, sisters Shirley Dunnagan, and Sue Bruce we made a trip to go see our sister Jeanne Engelmeier, 90 years old, in a nursing home. We were all devastated by what we saw. She had bruises on her arms hands and a black eye. She tried to get out of her bed and fell, then when she was in her wheelchair I guess she was trying to reach something on the floor and she fell with sitting in the wheelchair over and hit her head again.

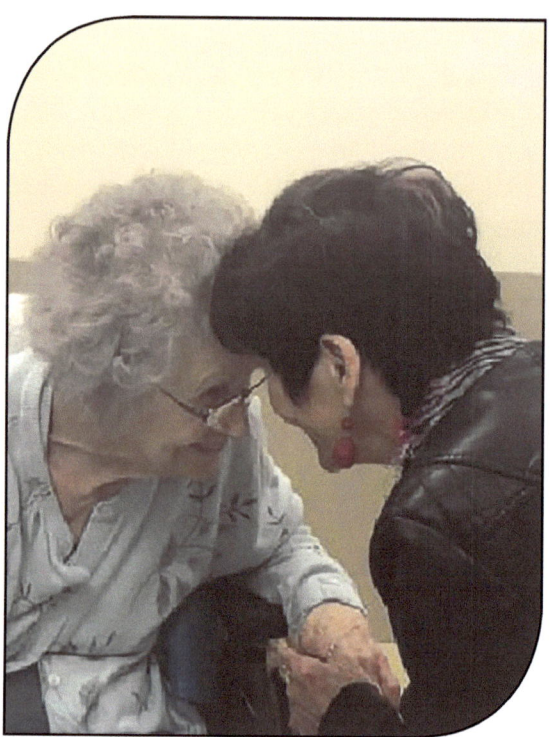

She was on antibiotics and other medicine, she slept in the wheelchair for a good time while we sit there till she woke up. It took a while for her to see us but I will say one thing she always knows my name. Jeanne and I went to cosmetology in Olney Illinois, home of the White Squirrels. God really is very kind to me, despite having Alzheimer's disease, she can still remember me – What a euphoric time I had!

After all the heartaches and faith-threatening circumstances, I realized the I have become stronger than I used to be. Though I cry sometimes, I have proven to my self that the strength I have is commendable. The extrinsic motivation I have from my friends and family made me realize such strength and how I can use it on my advantage.

I remember the time I mimed Jesus. Perhaps, Jesus' strength has already run in my veins, I just forget it but now it came back. I have loved God more and my faith grew even higher.

My life has been a roller coaster and I couldn't imagine how I was able to go through the obstacles and face the upside-down world.

The muddy course of my existence made me realize the people who are true and real. During the time of getting through the stroke I have experienced; I found the value of family and friends. After the thundering-shock news about Barbara's death, I realized the importance of time.

What added the pressure of depression and demotivation was the fact that during these impediments, the guy who I considered my comrade - didn't stay the same as I was expecting. It is really empirical that during the times of uncertainties and hurt, you would really find the real-attitude of a person. Though he was at my side during those moments; he just revealed his real self which made me sad, because the person I used to know was just a mock-up of someone I dreamt him to be.

> *"From Monday to Sunday, he became worse*
> *With tigered eyes, he pointed at me and curse.*
> *I asked him what's wrong,*
> *"I don't want to be with you anymore" - it*
> *echoed to me like a painful song "*

Knowing the real him isn't bad after all. It was just another mistake which I needed to fix. We both tried to carpenter the relationship, but it's just like a glass which cannot be formed back to its original face.

> *"From sunrise to sunset,*
> *I feel so upset.*
> *The bottle once full-now is empty.*
> *My guarded life - now no sentry"*

I was in pain knowing that I still haven't forgotten those mess I had faced - But a recent Judicial Separation had happened. This concluded that agony and suffering are really chasing after me, but I am up for the challenge and will never let it bring me down.

"It took me a month or two,
To realiz that I still have my family and friends too.
He is a broken piece of art,
And they are now the center of my broken heart "

"Truly everything happens for a reason,
Someone left me with ultimate treason.
But I dwelt on the positive side of a thing,
And to GOD I gave up everything."

"Seeing myself smile, makes me wonder about that hodad.
I hope he is happy now and again will never go mad.
He just lost a treasure his life could ever have.
But for you "my EX-comrade"; on my birthday, I will forgive
you and leave everything to GOD in heaven above."

"Center of my Broken Heart"
By: John Mark Lungay Tampus

I believe that God really never left me and just gave these hardships to get back to him. Though I was like a lost sheep, God still finds and never forget me as his child. And I couldn't be more grateful to have the family who introduced God to me.

    We were lucky to have great parents who taught us about God. My dad had bad diabetes but never missed work to take care of his kids. My mother was an angel every time my mom needed something so did one of us kids that mom always put herself behind and made sure we got it first. We were taught to treat people with love. We thought we didn't have much but always had food to eat, clean clothes to wear, a home to live in. So we had everything because we believed the God is everything.

    Besides having great parents and siblings, I am also ecstatic to have great and very loving kids who never left me when I thought everyone did. I know that my kids love me more than they love themselves, I just couldn't imagine how God showered and soaped me with so much love.

    God is almighty indeed! Incomparable and powerful!

    I have been so blessed with my Children Stacey and Rich, Amy and Tim, and Kenny. They have given me three children a piece and my Grandson Cole Lawson gave me a great-grandchild and another one on the way. I am a very blessed mother and grandmother.

    My deceased Husband Kenny Jamison died young and I'm sure he is looking down of all that he has missed.

    I am very blessed with all my family, my dear friends from school from First Grade to High School.

This book is not only to share my story but to also express my gratitude to the people who showed kindness and who have assisted throughout my healing process.

My son, Kenny, who has written a song entitled " **Anywhere with you**" when I had a stroke. I have been listening to this song to help me move forward.

He truly is a man of courage and love. Despite going through a divorce, he was still able to maintain composure and never ceased his faith to God. Perhaps, he got his motivation from his kids who he loves so much.

God has poured graces to him and now has joined a band called "**Flatliner**" where he can showcase his talent and be able to spread a message to the people through singing.

My 2 daughters who have been very successful in the career they have chosen also is one of the blessings I am more than thankful about. I am happy to know that they are also happy about their lives and that they are as well proud of me as their mom.

My Marketing and Publishing Executive, Toni Black, from MURLINK PRINT AND MEDIA. He is a kind man from the Philippines. I never thought that someone from the other country will be able to help me not only on my book project but also at times when I needed someone to talk to. Toni checks up on me from time to time, not to ask about my book project but just to ask me how's my day going. Such gestures made me consider him as my son. He is an intelligent person who helped me finish this book and who also reviewed the whole manuscript.

God led me to my publishing consultant Toni, I thank him for his expertise, kind spirit and passion to see this book come to fruition. His quickness to help and concern with the excellence of this Book calmed my soul and encouraged me greatly to the Lord. I am blessed in heart to call Toni a son of mine, through God and the wonderful friend and gift.

His Family who also I am grateful to know, has been supportive by making sure Toni will be able to finish and assist me throughout the process. I have seen his family which I found very sweet and gay.

I am not going to say a Stoke is easy, to me, it is a mean thing. Its definitely takes over your body. I have talked with stroke survivors many times and when I see someone that had a stroke, I will stop and talk to them because I can relate to how they feel.

I just want to say to all my family and many friends thank you for everything and being there for me. Even though I went through trials of bad depressions, bitterness and wanting to die, I realize that the devil tried so hard on me to stay in my bad thoughts. I give all the glory to my savior that I fought the battle. I only hope and pray that people going through bad times with their health or many other things that you will be able to rise above it. The thing that helped me was to have my faith and be positive and never give up.

"When life knocks you down, accept that everything happens for a reason. Feel the pain, cry like a wolf, start to move forward, learn from those experiences, smile as nothing happened, praise the Lord with all your heart, and expect that something might happen in just a blink of an eye."

– Mary Ellen Eaton Smith

Love to All!!

www.ingramcontent.com/pod-product-compliance
Ingram Content Group UK Ltd.
Pitfield, Milton Keynes, MK11 3LW, UK
UKHW061401260426
12048UKWH00054B/1